EVERYTHING SPORTS ALMANACS

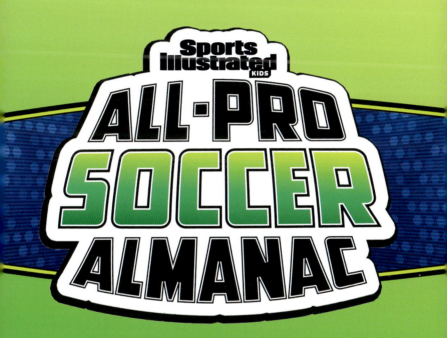

BY PATRICK DONNELLY

CAPSTONE PRESS
a capstone imprint

Published by Capstone Press, an imprint of Capstone
1710 Roe Crest Drive, North Mankato, Minnesota 56003
capstonepub.com

Copyright © 2026 by Capstone. All rights reserved. No part of this publication may be reproduced in whole or in part, or stored in a retrieval system, or transmitted in any form or by any means, electronic, mechanical, photocopying, recording, or otherwise, without written permission of the publisher.

SPORTS ILLUSTRATED KIDS is a trademark of ABG-SI LLC. Used with permission.

Library of Congress Cataloging-in-Publication Data
Names: Donnelly, Patrick, author.
Title: All-pro soccer almanac / by Patrick Donnelly.
Description: North Mankato, Minnesota : Capstone Press, 2026. | Series: Sports illustrated kids. Everything sports almanacs | Audience term: juvenile | Audience: Ages 8-11 Capstone Press | Audience: Grades 4-6 Capstone Press | Summary: "Exciting pro soccer facts in a variety of formats keep excited sports fans turning the pages."— Provided by publisher.
Identifiers: LCCN 2024055519 (print) | LCCN 2024055520 (ebook) | ISBN 9798875232909 (hardcover) | ISBN 9798875232855 (paperback) | ISBN 9798875232862 (pdf) | ISBN 9798875232879 (epub) | ISBN 9798875232886 (kindle edition)
Subjects: LCSH: Soccer—Miscellanea—Juvenile literature.
Classification: LCC GV943.25 .D665 2026 (print) | LCC GV943.25 (ebook) | DDC 796.334—dc23
LC record available at https://lccn.loc.gov/2024055519
LC ebook record available at https://lccn.loc.gov/2024055520

Quote Source:
p. 21, "Maradona, England and The Hand of God," published January 1, 2024, fifa.com/en/articles/diego-maradona-argentina-england-hand-of-god-1986, Accessed January 6, 2025

Editorial Credits
Editor: Mandy Robbins; Designer: Sarah Bennett; Media Researcher: Rebekah Hubstenberger; Production Specialist: Tori Abraham

Image Credits
Alamy: Cal Sport Media, 9 (bottom left); Associated Press: Ulrik Pedersen/NurPhoto, 29 (bottom); Getty Images: ALBERTO PIZZOLI/AFP, 18, Archivo El Grafico, 21, Azael Rodriguez, 34, Boris Streubel, 45, Central Press, 39, Dan Mullan, front cover (right), David Ramos, 37, 40, Duncan Raban/Allsport, 8 (middle left), Eric Alonso, 30-31, 38, FRANCK FIFE/AFP, 13, funnybank, 14, Gonzalo Arroyo Moreno, front cover (top), Hulton Archive, 12, iStock/Fourleaflover (country flags), 5, 10, 11, Kevin C. Cox, 35, Laurence Griffiths, 17, 26, Matthias Hangst, 6, 29 (bottom), Michael Regan, 4, Pedro Vilela, 29 (top), Sean M. Haffey, front cover (left), Shaun Botterill, 10, Shaun Botterill/Allsport, 28, Thorsten Wagner, 15 (bottom), Tim Keeton - Pool, 23, Valerio Pennicino, 47; Newscom: Mirrorpix, 24; Shutterstock: Arrobani Studio (gold background), 25, 38, Fallen Knight (holographic background), cover and throughout, Far700, 32 (tv), Foxy Fox, 20, Gethuk_Studio (hexagon shape), throughout, Igor Link, 44, kulyk, 43, lefthanderman, 41, 46 (soccer ball), MariaLev, 27 (club logos), Maya Raab, 32 (Brazil scene tv screen), mentalmind (stars, medals and trophies), 25, 26, 27, Mikolaj Barbanell, 11, NOMONARTS, 5, Olga Moonlight (soccer ball background), 3, 7, 48, Otviart, 46 (magic background), Panatphong, 19, Ringo Chiu, 8 (bottom right), Sportoakimirka, 9 (top left), StarLine, back cover (soccer background); Sports Illustrated: Erick W. Rasco, 42, Jerry Cooke, 33, Robert Beck, 15 (top), Simon Bruty, 22

Any additional websites and resources referenced in this book are not maintained, authorized, or sponsored by Capstone. All product and company names are trademarks™ or registered® trademarks of their respective holders.

All stats are current through March 12, 2025.

Printed and bound in the USA. 006307

Table of Contents

About the Leagues 4

Greatest Games 12

Standout Plays 18

Team Dynasties 24

Iconic Players 32

Record Breakers 40

About the Leagues

BASICS OF WORLD SOCCER

The top men's soccer leagues have been around for 100 years or more. Women's soccer has surged in popularity since the 1990s. The top pro leagues are in Europe. Star players from around the world play there. Countries outside of Europe have their own leagues too.

EUROPEAN LEAGUES

England
Premier League

Germany
Bundesliga

Italy
Serie A

Spain
La Liga

France
Ligue 1

WHO'S IN CHARGE?
Each continent has a governing body for soccer. Europe's is called the Union of European Football Associations (UEFA). The top clubs from all over Europe compete in the UEFA Champions League.

MOST TITLES BY CLUB
IN TOP FIVE EUROPEAN LEAGUES

LEAGUE AND COUNTRY	CLUB	NUMBER OF TITLES
La Liga/Spain Founded in 1929	Real Madrid	36
Serie A/Italy Founded in 1898	Juventus	36
Bundesliga/Germany Founded in 1963	Bayern Munich	33
Premier League/England Founded in 1992	Manchester United	13
Ligue 1/France Founded in 1932	Paris Saint-Germain	12

Double Identity!

Most soccer stars play for two teams—a professional club and a national team. Professional teams pay their players. National teams represent countries in the Olympics and the World Cup.

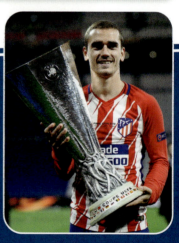

»Antoine Griezmann's team, Atletico Madrid, won the UEFA Europa League final in 2018. He also plays for the French National Team.

UP AND DOWN THE LADDER

Most countries have levels of soccer leagues. One term used for it is a ladder.

Teams can move up and down the ladder depending on where they finish in their league each season.

The three teams at the bottom of the standings drop down a league the next season. They are replaced by the top three teams from the lower league.

Teams can only move one level each season.

U.S. LEAGUE HISTORY

The United States took a while to warm to soccer, but its popularity continues to grow. The country has had two major men's soccer leagues.

The first was the North American Soccer League (NASL). It began in 1968 and lasted until 1984. The second is Major League Soccer (MLS). That was founded in 1996.

» **Top photo:** The New York Cosmos take on the Fort Lauderdale Strikers in a 1980 NASL match.

» **Bottom photo:** Los Angeles FC plays Austin FC in a 2024 MLS match.

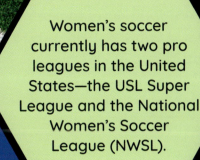

Women's soccer currently has two pro leagues in the United States—the USL Super League and the National Women's Soccer League (NWSL).

WOMEN RULE THE PITCH!

Of the two leagues, the NWSL is the most competitive. TV viewership of NWSL games rose more than 500 percent in 2024!

»Left photo: Trinity Rodman is a rising star in the NWSL. The forward for the Washington Spirit became the youngest NWSL player to notch 10 goals and 10 assists. She was just shy of her 21st birthday.

The **WORLD CUP** is the **BIGGEST PRIZE** in international soccer. The top national teams gather every four years to see who's the best. The first World Cup was held in 1930. The Women's World Cup began in 1991.

» Italian players celebrate their 2006 World Cup final win.

MOST MEN'S WORLD CUP TITLES

5	4	4	3
Brazil	Germany/ West Germany	Italy	Argentina

WOMEN'S WORLD CUP TITLES

4 **2**
United States Germany

1 **1** **1**
Norway Japan Spain

»Team USA celebrates their 2019 World Cup final victory.

Greatest Games

ENGLAND'S 1966 WORLD CUP WIN

England is the birthplace of soccer, but its national team has struggled in big tournaments. The 1966 World Cup was different. England reached the final against West Germany. The score was tied 2-2 through 90 minutes.

English striker Geoff Hurst (shown above left) fired a shot 11 minutes into extra time. The ball struck the crossbar and shot straight down to the goal line. The rules state that the whole ball has to cross the line for the goal to count. The Germans argued that point, but the officials called it a goal. Hurst scored again in the game's final minute. England had a 4-2 win for its first, and still only, World Cup.

WORLD CUP SHOOT-OUTS

There have been just three penalty shoot-outs in Men's World Cup finals history:

- In 1994, Brazil beat Italy.
- In 2006, Italy defeated France.
- In 2022, Argentina beat France.

»Gonzalo Montiel of Argentina scores past French goalkeeper Hugo Lloris in the 2022 World Cup final.

1999 WOMEN'S WORLD CUP FINAL

The third Women's World Cup was played in the United States. The host team faced China in the final game. After 120 minutes of play, neither team had scored.

The teams went to a penalty shoot-out. U.S. goalkeeper Briana Scurry made a diving save on one of China's shots. The other four players scored. The first four U.S. players scored too. That left it up to U.S. midfielder Brandi Chastain. She fired hard to the right. The ball zoomed into the back of the net. The United States won!

» Goalkeeper Briana Scurry (in blue) and teammates celebrate their Women's World Cup final victory.

Japan's Cup Win

In 2011, the United States and Japan battled to a 2-2 draw in the Women's World Cup final. Japan won the shoot-out 3-1 to win its first title.

WHAT'S A TWO-LEGGED TIE?

When some tournaments reach the knockout round, a winner is decided by a two-legged tie. That's when the teams play twice—once in each team's stadium. The team with the most total goals advances.

BARCELONA'S
TWO-LEGGED TIE
CHAMPIONS LEAGUE
COMEBACK

FC Barcelona faced Paris Saint-Germain (PSG) in the 2017 UEFA Champions League. The first leg in Paris was a blowout. PSG beat Barcelona 4–0.

Back on home turf, the Spaniards scored three times in the first 50 minutes. Then PSG added a goal. That made the total score 5–3.

Barcelona didn't give up. Neymar tied it up with a score and a penalty kick. Finally, during stoppage time, Neymar sent a long crossing pass toward the PSG net. A sliding Sergi Roberto kicked the ball into the net. Barcelona had a stunning 6–5 victory!

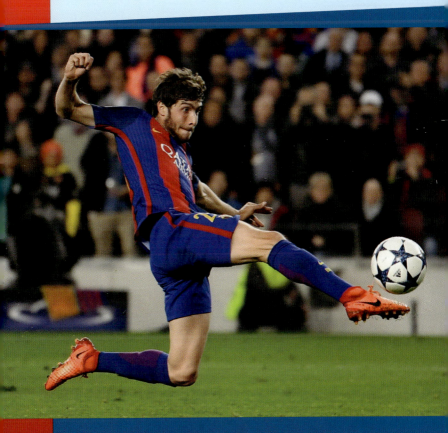

» Sergi Roberto scores Barcelona's sixth goal of the two-legged round, securing Barcelona's victory over Paris Saint-Germain.

Standout Plays

RONALDO'S BICYCLE KICK

In a 2018 European Champions League game, Real Madrid was attacking against Juventus. Cristiano Ronaldo hung out near the Juventus net. Teammate Dani Carvajal lofted a high pass near Ronaldo.

In one smooth move, Ronaldo leaped with his back to the goal. His foot kicked the ball while it was over his head. The ball rocketed into the net. The crowd roared! Ronaldo's bicycle kick became an instant classic.

RAPINOE TO WAMBACH

The United States trailed Brazil 2–1 in the final seconds of the 2011 Women's World Cup semifinals. Megan Rapinoe took a pass on the left side from Carli Lloyd. Then Rapinoe launched a long pass toward the Brazil goal. Abby Wambach leaped and headed it into the net. The United States then won a penalty shoot-out to win the game.

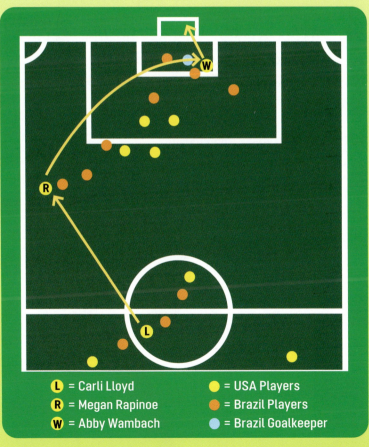

THE 'HAND OF GOD' GOAL

In the 1986 World Cup quarterfinals, Argentina faced England. Diego Maradona, Argentina's star striker, tried to pass to a teammate at the top of England's penalty area.

The ball popped up. Maradona and English goalkeeper Peter Shilton both jumped for it. The ball bounced off of Maradona and into the net. If Maradona's hand had touched it, it would have been illegal. Officials ruled the ball bounced off his head, so the goal was legal. At the time, there was no instant replay. If there had been, the refs would have seen that the ball *did* touch his hand.

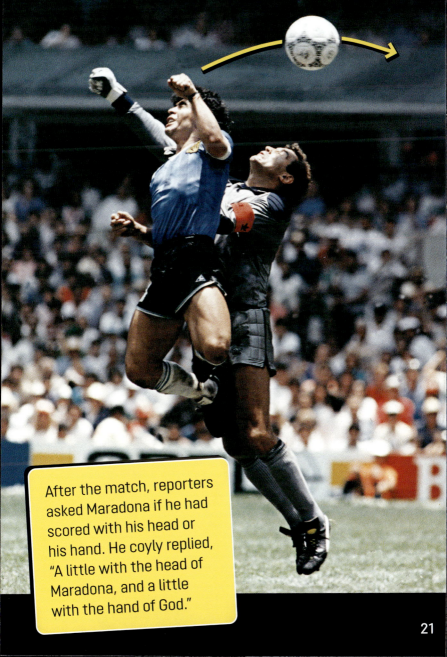

After the match, reporters asked Maradona if he had scored with his head or his hand. He coyly replied, "A little with the head of Maradona, and a little with the hand of God."

GOALKEEPER ON OFFENSE!

It's rare for a goalkeeper to score, but U.S. legend Tim Howard did it in 2012. Deep in his own end, Howard swung big with his right leg. The wind pushed the ball down the field. The ball bounced over the goalkeeper's head and into the net.

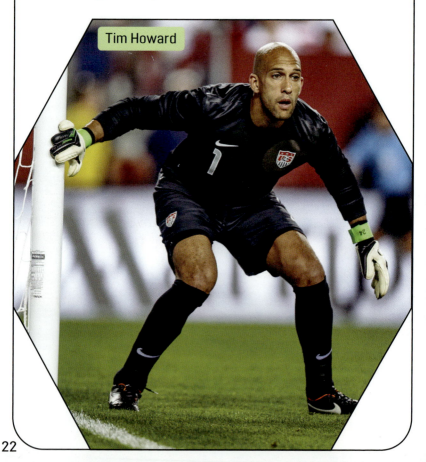

Tim Howard

PREMIER LEAGUE GOALKEEPER GOALS

Peter Schmeichel
Aston Villa vs. Everton, October 20, 2001

Brad Friedel
Blackburn Rovers vs. Charlton, February 21, 2004

Paul Robinson
Tottenham Hotspur vs. Watford, March 17, 2007

Tim Howard
Everton vs. Bolton, January 4, 2012

Asmir Begović
Stoke City vs. Southampton, November 2, 2013

Alisson
Liverpool vs. West Brom, May 16, 2021

» In the final seconds of the match, Alisson (#1 in black kit) heads the ball into the net to notch the game-winning goal.

Team Dynasties

SIR ALEX FERGUSON AND MANCHESTER UNITED

No English club has dominated more than Manchester United under manager Sir Alex Ferguson. He led the team from 1986 to 2013. His teams won more than 30 trophies.

» Ferguson shouts instructions to his players.

Ferguson's teams won 13 Premier League titles . . .

. . . and two UEFA Champions League finals.

He was named the Premier League Manager of the Year 11 times.

25

PEP GUARDIOLA'S TROPHY CASE

Pep Guardiola is one of the most successful managers in soccer history. He won multiple titles during his time with Barcelona (2008–2012), Bayern Munich (2013–2016), and Manchester City (2016–).

»FC Barcelona players toss manager Pep Guardiola in the air to celebrate a Champions League victory.

BARCELONA TROPHIES

2009	La Liga
2009	Champions League
2010	La Liga
2011	La Liga
2011	Champions League

BAYERN MUNICH TROPHIES

2014	Bundesliga
2015	Bundesliga
2016	Bundesliga

MANCHESTER CITY TROPHIES

2018	Premier League
2019	Premier League
2021	Premier League
2022	Premier League
2023	Premier League
2023	Champions League
2024	Premier League

Brazil's World Cup Success

The World Cup has been played every four years since 1930, except for a gap around World War II (1939-1945). Only one country has captured five championships—Brazil.

Brazil's winning streak started in 1958, when a teenager named Pelé helped win its first title. Four years later, Brazil won again. They won their third title in 1970. That was Pelé's last match for Brazil. But the dynasty continued. Brazil won the World Cup in 1994 and again in 2002.

»1994 FIFA World Cup champs!

Neymar

BRAZIL'S LEADING SCORERS

Neymar	79 goals (128 matches)
Pelé	77 goals (92 matches)
Ronaldo	62 goals (98 matches)
Romário	55 goals (70 matches)
Zico	48 goals (71 matches)

* Goals scored for Brazil in national team matches only

WHO TRAILS BRAZIL IN WORLD CUP STANDINGS?

4	Italy
4	Germany/West Germany
3	Argentina
2	Uruguay
2	France
1	England
1	Spain

»French players celebrate their 2018 World Cup championship.

RIVALRY!
REAL MADRID VS. FC BARCELONA

Two clubs in Spain's La Liga have become international giants. At the end of the 2024 season, Real Madrid had won 36 La Liga titles. Barcelona had won 27.

The rivalry between these teams has its very own name—El Clásico. The competition dates back to 1902. Barcelona won the first meeting. But as of 2024, Real Madrid led the rivalry with 106 wins to Barcelona's 100 wins. There have also been 51 draws.

» The teams play twice a year. Fans pack the stadiums.

MOST GOALS IN EL CLÁSICO

26	Lionel Messi, Barcelona
18	Cristiano Ronaldo, Real Madrid
18	Alfredo Di Stéfano, Real Madrid
16	Karim Benzema, Real Madrid
15	Raúl, Real Madrid
14	César Rodríguez, Barcelona
14	Paco Gento, Real Madrid
14	Ferenc Puskás, Real Madrid
12	Santillana, Real Madrid
11	Luis Suárez, Barcelona

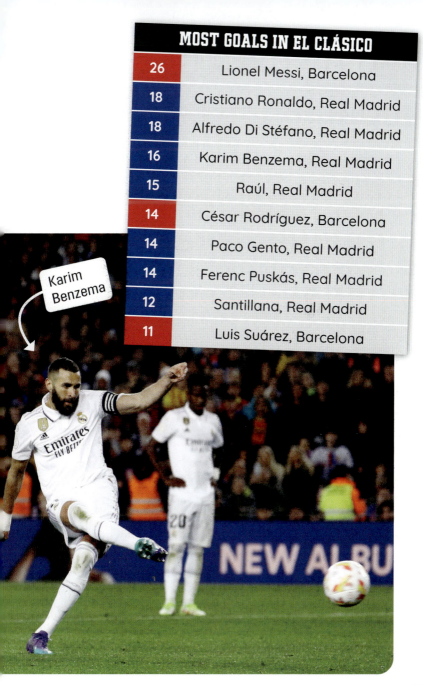

Karim Benzema

Iconic Players

PELÉ! Few athletes have impacted their sport more than Pelé. The striker from Brazil took the world by storm in 1958. At just 17 years old, he led his country to the World Cup championship. It was the first year the tournament was televised all around the world. Pelé scored three goals in the semifinals against France and two in the final against Sweden.

In 1962 and 1970, Pelé led Brazil to two more World Cup titles. He ended his career with the New York Cosmos in the NASL. His time with the Cosmos helped make soccer popular in the United States.

»Pelé vies for the ball in a 1975 NASL game.

Most Career Goals for U.S. Women's National Team

The United States has been the world's most successful women's national team. They've had many outstanding goal scorers along the way.

Can you match these top goal scorers to the number of goals they scored?

Kristine Lilly
Carli Lloyd
Abby Wambach
Mia Hamm
Alex Morgan

158 **130**
123 **134**
184

ANSWERS: Abby Wambach 184, Mia Hamm 158, Carli Lloyd 134, Kristine Lilly 130, Alex Morgan 123

QUIZ: How Well Do You Know Christine Sinclair?

1. How many years was Christine Sinclair Canada's top women's soccer player?

2. How many goals did Sinclair score in that time?

3. How many Women's World Cups did Sinclair play in?

4. What year did Sinclair help Canada win an Olympic gold medal?

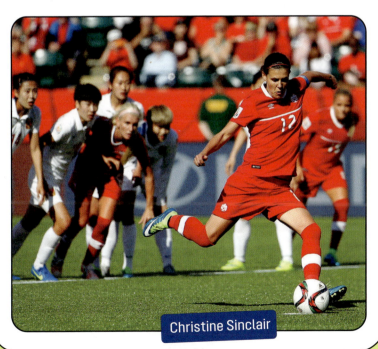

Christine Sinclair

ANSWERS: 1. 23 **2.** 190—more than any player, male or female, in international play **3.** 6 **4.** 2021

MESSI
VS.
RONALDO

Two of the greatest players in soccer history have had a fierce rivalry. Argentina's Lionel Messi has top-notch dribbling and scoring skills. Cristiano Ronaldo of Portugal scores incredible goals, many off free kicks.

Messi joined FC Barcelona in 2004. He led La Liga in goals eight times. In 2022, he led Argentina to its first World Cup title in 36 years. Meanwhile, Ronaldo was a star in the top leagues of England, Spain, and Italy. He scored his 900th total goal while playing for Portugal in 2024.

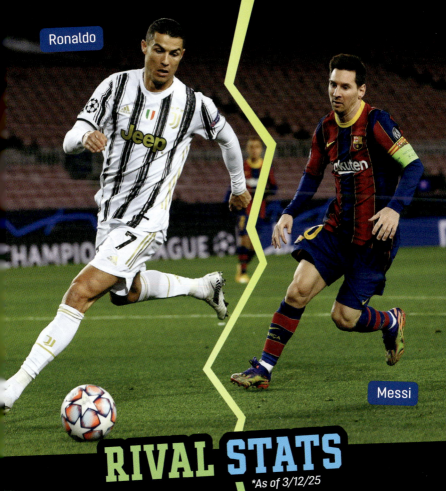

RIVAL STATS
As of 3/12/25

Total Goals
Ronaldo 927 • Messi 852

International Goals
Ronaldo 135 • Messi 112

Matches
Ronaldo 1,268 • Messi 1,086

Ballon d'Or wins
Messi 8 • Ronaldo 5

Assists
Messi 381 • Ronaldo 257

BALLON D'OR

The TOP PLAYER in the world each season is awarded the Ballon d'Or.

The FIRST WINNER was England's Stanley Matthews in 1956.

Lionel Messi set the RECORD with eight wins.

The Ballon d'Or Féminin has been awarded to the TOP WOMEN'S PLAYER since 2018.

Alexia Putellas of Spain is the FIRST player to WIN it TWICE.

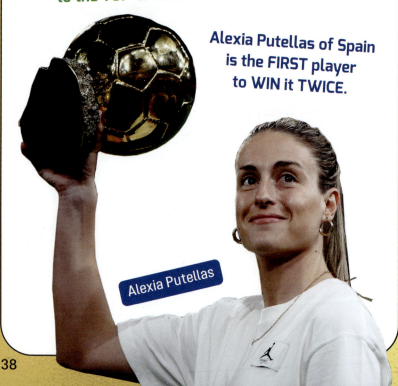

Alexia Putellas

PUSKÁS AWARD

Ferenc Puskás was a short, stocky striker from Hungary, known for bold runs through the defense. He helped Real Madrid win three championships and five straight La Liga titles in the 1950s and 1960s. Today, the Puskás Award goes to the player with the "most beautiful" goal each year.

Ferenc Puskás

Record Breakers

MESSI'S 91 GOALS

Lionel Messi holds many records. But 2012 was his banner year. While playing for Barcelona and the Argentina national team, Messi scored 91 goals. That's more than any player has ever scored in a calendar year.

Messi

Messi got started on January 15, 2012, when he scored two goals in Barcelona's 4–2 victory over Real Betis. He went on to score **79 goals** in 60 matches for his club team.

Meanwhile, he appeared in nine matches for Argentina, scoring **12 goals**.

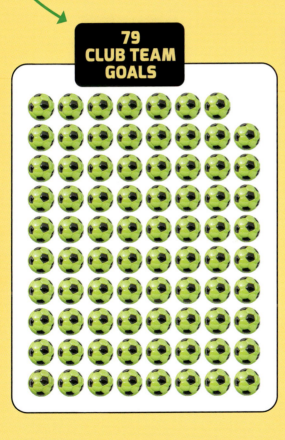

MARTA!

Few women's soccer players have combined the speed, skill, and scoring touch of Brazil's Marta. Girls' soccer was not popular in Brazil when she was growing up, so Marta played with the boys.

In 2002, at age 14, she made her debut with Brazil's women's national team. In 2003, she played in her first Women's World Cup. Overall, Marta scored 17 goals in six Women's World Cups. That's more than any other player—male or female.

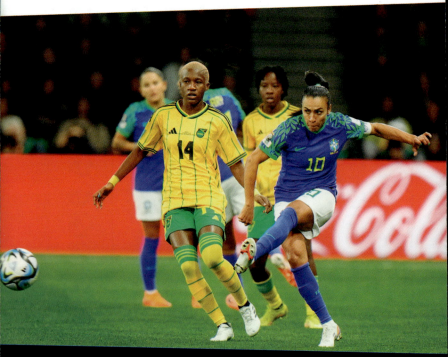

»Marta (right) in the 2023 Women's World Cup

MOST WORLD CUP GOALS

17 GOALS
Marta, Brazil

16 GOALS
Miroslav Klose, Germany

15 GOALS
Ronaldo, Brazil

14 GOALS
Birgit Prinz, Germany
Abby Wambach, USA
Gerd Müller, West Germany

13 GOALS
Just Fontaine, France

Arsenal's Invincibles

Only one team has gone an entire Premier League season without a loss. In the 2003–2004 season, Arsenal finished with 26 wins, 12 draws, and zero losses. "The Invincibles" won the league title by 11 points over second-place Chelsea.

Arsenal's 2003–2004 Starting Lineup

GOALKEEPER
Jens Lehmann

MIDFIELDERS
Robert Pires
Gilberto Silva
Patrick Vieira
Fredrik Ljungberg

DEFENDERS
Ashley Cole
Sol Campbell
Kolo Touré
Lauren

FORWARDS
Thierry Henry
Dennis Bergkamp

Almost Impossible

It's almost impossible for a team to score five goals in nine minutes. It's even more unlikely for one player to score all five goals. But on September 22, 2015, Bayern Munich's Robert Lewandowski scored five times between the 51st and 60th minutes against Wolfsburg.

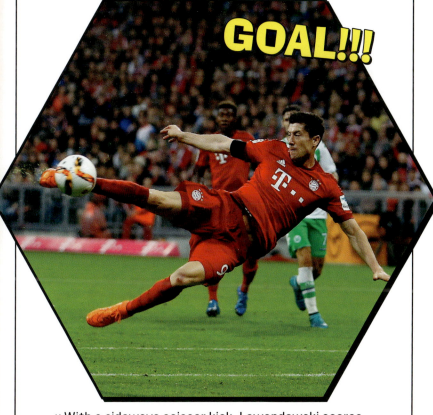

»With a sideways scissor kick, Lewandowski scores the fifth goal of his record-breaking match.

What's a Hat Trick?

A hat trick is a rare feat in soccer. It happens when a player scores three goals in the same game.

MOST HAT TRICKS SINCE 2000	
66	Cristiano Ronaldo
59	Lionel Messi
35	Ali Ashfaq
33	Robert Lewandowski
30	Luis Suárez
27	Ali Mabkhout
26	Vjatšeslav Zahovaiko

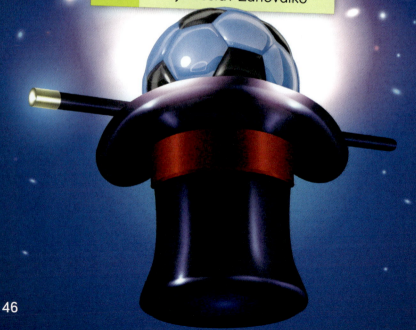

What's a Clean Sheet?

In soccer, a shutout is often called a "clean sheet." Goalkeepers earn a clean sheet when they keep the other team from scoring for a full game.

MOST CAREER CLEAN SHEETS	
501	Gianluigi Buffon
440	Edwin van der Sar
440	Iker Casillas
397	Petr Čech
358	Pepe Reina

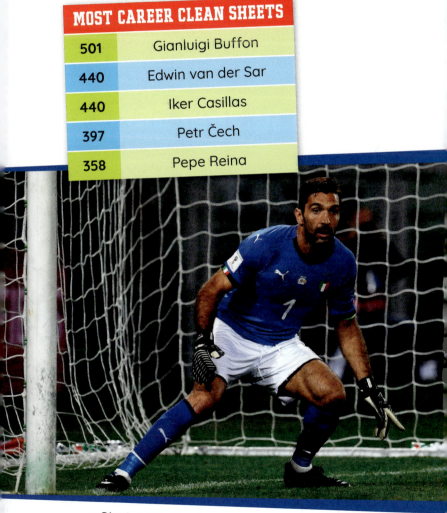

» Gianluigi Buffon is the king of clean sheets.

About the Author

Patrick Donnelly is a sportswriter and author who lives in Minneapolis, Minnesota. He's written more than 100 books about sports. He also frequently covers Minnesota sports teams for the Associated Press.

More in This Series

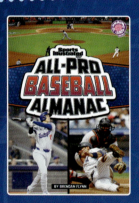

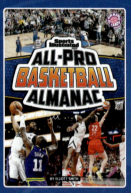

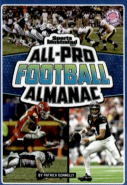

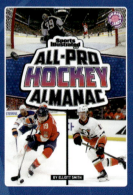